My Unique Design Works

Reflecting the uniqueness in you!

Natalie Shanel Watts

MUDWorks - My Unique Design Works

Copyright © 2013

Published by Younique Design, Inc.
Crete, IL 60417

Unless otherwise noted, all Scripture quotations are taken from the New International Version of the Bible

This book makes references and quotes from the movie, The Wiz.
Lumet, Sidney (Director). 1978 (Year). The Wiz [Film]. Location: Motown Productions

This book uses information obtained through personal training in the personalities from CLASSeminars, Inc.

Library of Congress Control Number: 2013939689

All rights reserved under International Copyright Law. No part of this book may be reproduced or transmitted in any form or by any means, electronic or mechanical, including photocopying and recording, or by an information storage and retrieval system, without permission in writing from the author or publisher.

ISBN: 978-0-9831339-2-6

Printed in the United States of America

1st Edition

~ Oops! ~

Although we worked hard to make this book perfect and avoid mistakes, reality is, people are not perfect and this book may not be either. However, we respectfully ask that you do not allow mistakes or your preferred writing style to block you from the message that God wants you to receive. Enjoy the journey.

~ Quotes ~

"If the world was perfect, it wouldn't be."
~ Yogi Berra

"If you're not making mistakes, then you're not doing anything. I'm positive that a doer makes mistakes."
~ John Wooden

"Shoot for the moon and if you miss you will be among the stars."
~ Les Brown

"Not that I have already obtained all this, or have already been made perfect, but I press on to take hold of that for which Christ Jesus took hold of me."
~ Paul, Philippians 3:12

~ Creative Liberty ~

We have taken the creative liberty to use the British style of writing in some cases when it pertains to punctuation outside of quotation marks for special phrases. Additionally, we have chosen to use a passive voice in some cases, and switch between 1st, 2nd, & 3rd voices throughout the journey of communicating the message.

The MUD Works Experience

I attended a Mudworks workshop in order to better understand my personality and how it works. As I learned about the different personality types' strengths and weaknesses, I began to be more confident about my uniqueness. Natalie was gracious to give me help with a situation that I was having on my job. She identified the personality type vs. mine and how I could better communicate. This was not only helpful but stress relieving. Thank you Natalie, I am looking forward to learning more.
S.B.

~

Natalie really helped me understand the different personality styles. After putting a few to the test, I was able to communicate with others in ways that I had not before. It felt good to sit and converse with others and really feel their hearts. I believe Natalie has found her niche and very qualified to represent **MUD** *Works*.
G.F.

~

My wife and I attended a **MUD** *Works* workshop. What stood out most for me was a question a gentleman asked about how Cholerics and Phlegmatics are able to co-exist. In response to this question, and many more, Natalie's insight and understanding of the personality types provided a new fresh outlook for everybody in the room. I really enjoyed Natalie's point, which explained while we all share different traits we should not allow them to become overly excessive behaviors where we are not able to work together.
E.M.

~

Natalie related information in a way that considered how all the four personalities could receive the information she was sharing. I watched as people were enlightened about their own dominant personality types as well as their spouse's characteristics. All around the room you could hear people saying, "Oooohhh! Wow! Yep, that's me!" Couples left empowered in their relationships and enlightened by the perspective that Natalie shared. She valued individuals in a way that many couples had not experienced in that way before.
A.M.

The MUDWorks Experience

Natalie has the ability to address a large audience while reaching individuals on a personal level. Natalie is a private tutor amidst the crowd. She reads her audience, deciphers needs and provides clarification on key points.

When Natalie first spoke to me about the personality styles, I believed I was a Popular Sanguine. With her help, I was able to identify additional elements of who I am, such as my appreciation for loyalty, along with other attributes that allowed me to recognize and embrace my Powerful Choleric "doer." Natalie's teaching encouraged me to temper my natural impulse to "do" in order to provide my husband, a Peaceful Phlegmatic, with more opportunities to reflect.

What I most appreciate about Natalie's breadth of understanding is her belief that each individual is a unique treasure. Her primary focus is to make sure that we do not put one another into a box. Natalie sees people as people, not categories. Thank goodness for her refreshing perspective! She stresses the importance of self-realization to enhance our interaction with others. One specific self-realization came to me from the statement, "sometimes people think I mean it, when I am really joking." This is a true statement for me, which points to the Powerful Choleric tendencies. Through Natalie's teaching, I am able to see that as I become more aware of who I am—with a conscious effort to communicate more effectively—people will read my heart better.
E.R.

~

Mrs. Watts did a dynamic job with explaining the four personality styles with the group. These were Perfect Melancholy, Popular Sanguine, Powerful Choleric, and Peaceful Phlegmatic. With her ability to share the unique differences of each style with such clarity, we found it very easy to recognize traits that we possess. I learned that my most dominate personality style is the Perfect Melancholy and my husband's is the Powerful Choleric. As we continue to talk about the evening, both my husband and I seem to understand one another better. Learning about our personality styles definitely gives us a better appreciation for one another. It was most helpful to learn that our spouses do not do things to us with the intention to spite us, but because that happens to be how they are hardwired. We believe anyone who would attend an event where Mrs. Watts teaches on the four personality styles will leave with information that they can utilize in all types of relationships.
D. H. & D.H.

"Before I formed you in the womb I knew you, before you were born I set you apart; I appointed you as a prophet to the nations."

"Alas, Sovereign Lord," I said, "I do not know how to speak; I am too young." But the Lord said to me, "Do not say, 'I am too young.' You must go to everyone I send you to and say whatever I command you. Do not be afraid of them, for I am with you and will rescue you," declares the Lord. Then the Lord reached out his hand and touched my mouth and said to me, "I have put my words in your mouth."
(Jeremiah 1:5-10)

~

"He who has ears to hear, let him hear."
(Matthew 11:15)

Table of Contents

Preface   3

Introduction ~ Reflection   5

Spittle #1
The Yellow Brick Road (the journey)   7

Spittle #2
I Was Blind, But Now I See   15

Spittle #3
MUD *Works* - *M*y *U*nique *D*esign *Works*!   21

Spittle #4
Toil Your Soil   29

Spittle #5
Yard Crashers   35

Spittle #6
Love   37

Preface

MUD *Works* is an acronym for *My Unique Design Works*! I discovered that *"my unique design works"* once I was introduced and certified in the study of *the 4 basic personalities*. Understanding *the personalities* has had an influential impact in my life and allows me to see beyond the surface of myself and others. Often I relate to the blind man whom Jesus healed when he spat on the ground, made mud spittle and anointed the man's eyes. Jesus told the man to, "Go wash in the pool of Siloam." And when the man obeyed these instructions and washed, he became a man who could see. For me, the mud made of spittle is symbolic of my eyes being anointed with the understanding of *the personalities*.

Understanding *the personalities* stimulated an internal growth process, as questions were answered about me. I was able to better understand how other people saw me as well, when before it befuddled me. I later learned to adapt myself to the different personality temperaments in order to be more effective. I'm no longer confused, but realize everyone has a perspective through the lenses from which they view life, which is connected to their personality temperament. I now feel extremely confident in who God created me to be after being introduced to this study.

Not that I have already obtained all this, or have already arrived at my goal, but I press on to take hold of that for which Christ Jesus took hold of me. Brothers and sisters, I do not consider myself yet to have taken hold of it. But one thing I do: Forgetting what is behind and straining toward what is ahead, I press on toward the goal to win the prize for which God has called me heavenward in Christ Jesus. (Philippians 3:12-14, NIV)

Through this journey, I hope you will be able to see and understand yourself, as well as others. This book is broken into six parts, symbolic of the sixth day in which God created mankind. Each part is referred to as *Spittle* (spit or saliva often referenced in the Bible as a healing agent). My hope is that each *Spittle* will open your eyes and give you new perspectives and confidence to believe, **MUD** *Works* - *My Unique Design Works*!

I was blind, but now I see, and I hope to transfer the anointing so that you can see too; see yourself and others in ways you have never seen before.

Introduction

Reflection

Often I am described as a reflective person; stopping to think about myself or a situation I have encountered. Considering various angles, I decide if I should do things differently moving forward. I believe this is a healthy part of growth and development. As I approached a pivotal point in life, God placed me on a journey and helped me to see; everything in my life has been part of the process as He has unfolded and revealed me to myself. It has been a discovery, and reflecting shows me the world and my purpose in it. My reflection brings me face to face with myself, my relationships, and God.

Reflecting has been a journey of digging deep into the roots of my soul to discover my passions and my convictions. As I see who I am, I learn to take ownership of my own feelings and deal with myself accordingly; instead of displacing my feelings on others, which leads to unresolved offenses. The reflection not only gives me confidence in how God designed me, but also, somehow, serves as a mirror; allowing others to see themselves as well.

A reflection is defined as the change in direction of a wavefront at an interface between two different media so that the wavefront returns into the medium from which it originated.[1] When you reflect, the journey allows you to come to yourself and see just how God originally designed you to be, and how your design causes a particular reflection/reaction from another based on the characteristics of their design. In other words, depending on what your personality exudes, will reflect how another personality sees and react to you.

Sometimes it is hard to look at our reflection closely, because naturally we attract to what is attractive. We naturally don't desire to see or deal with the things we don't admire about ourselves. I encourage you to not be afraid of your reflection. It's a gift from God that reveals your strengths, weakness, and knowledge on how to develop and position your personality in relation to Him and others.

Spittle #1

THE YELLOW BRICK ROAD

The Journey with the 4 Personalities

One of my favorite movies is *The Wiz* - a musical with music and lyrics by Charlie Smalls (book by William F. Brown). It is a retelling of L. Frank Baum's *The Wonderful Wizard of Oz* in the context of African-American culture. A film adaptation was released in 1978 and I was introduced to it at a very young age. I have always connected with the film. God has always spoken to me through this film as I relate to the main character, Dorothy, and her journey to discovering self. While my goal is not to promote nor give a commentary on the movie, I will reference some key characters to introduce *the 4 basic personalities*; the fundamental lesson in my journey to discovering myself and my purpose.

On this journey, the main character, Dorothy, finds herself in the unfamiliar Land of Oz. She must travel *the yellow brick road* to the Emerald City to meet the Wiz who will get her back home. As she travels *the yellow brick road,* she acquires 3 friends (personalities) much different than herself.... or so it seems. And, they all are in need of something. All four of them later realize they already possessed their greatest needs/desires within themselves after going through the journey. In my opinion, Dorothy and her friends - Scarecrow, Tin Man, and Lion - reflect *the 4 basic personalities.*

Though we are created unique and different, there are general similarities that allow us to be grouped into four categories based on our personality temperaments. The study of the differences and interrelationship of these four categories are called *the Personalities* and each of us has a basic inborn personality that is predetermined before birth according to research. All personality-typing programs originate from this four basic personality study first established by Hippocrates, a Greek philosopher and physician, over 2400 years ago.

As you journey through this *Spittle*, reflect on the family, friends, and associates whom you have encountered in your own walk of life. Allow every person you encounter in your life's journey to be an opportunity to sharpen self, as you learn to glean from the strengths of *the Personalities* that are different from yours, while learning to position yourself to be an influence to them as well. *As iron sharpens iron, so one person sharpens another.* (Proverbs 27:17, NIV)

The Yellow Brick Road

YELLOW
Yellow symbolizes wisdom. Yellow means joy and happiness. People of high intellect favor yellow.

Yellow Energy; Like the energy of a bright sunny day, yellow brings **clarity and awareness**.

Pure, bright and sunny yellow is the easiest color to see. People who are **blind to other colors can usually see yellow**. Yellow is full of creative and intellectual energy.[1]

BRICK
Bricks are made from dried earth, usually from clay-bearing **subsoil**, and have been regarded as one of the longest lasting and strongest building materials used throughout history. [2]

As you travel *the yellow brick road* encountering people and discovering self, remember you are walking a long lasting, strong road with God who is creatively, with daily clarity and awareness, revealing yourself to you. He will pour His wisdom into you as you embrace what is your unique design, and allow the mud to cleanse you from those things that are not. Enjoy the journey!

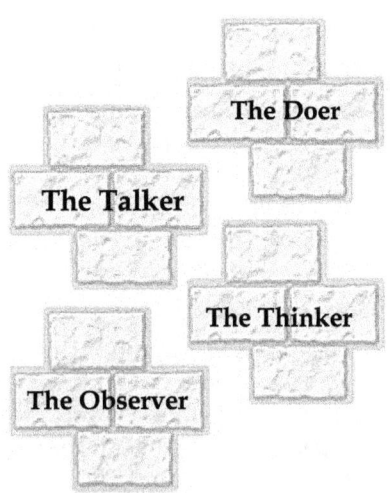

The 4 Personalities

Has anyone ever said to you,
"Does anything ever bother you?"
Or, "You know you play too much!"
Do you know those that talk with a touch?

Or maybe you may know someone
That seems like they do not have fun
They always want to work, no play
And always have a busy day.

"You think you know everything!"
Is a song that some may sing
Or do you say, "Things will be ok."
While others say, "If they do it my way!"

Has anyone ever said to you,
"Consider other's feelings too."
Or "It does not take all that!"
Then there are those that always chitchat

Do people tell you to put a smile on your face,
And others talk in your personal space?
Or do you ever wonder why
There are those that tend to cry?

Well here is a chance to catch a clue
As you learn you and others too
It's all around you, you will see
The 4 Basic Personalities

Dorothy (Phlegmatic Personality Characteristics)

Dorothy's need is to believe in herself. But she does not realize this, as she yearns to be back at home where there is *familiarity* and *comfort*. She is perceived as *shy* because she is *quiet* and at the beginning of the movie, before her *yellow brick road* journey begins, she expresses to herself her *disconnect* with what her family is feeling. She admits that the feeling is more than she can deal with. This reminds me of some Phlegmatics in my life, who have graced me the opportunity to see inside the mind and heart of the Phlegmatic - *"We have feelings, but if it's more than we can deal with, we would rather not; nor deal with the feelings of another because it is too much drama and disturbs the peace and comfort we strive to have within."* (paraphrased)

Her aunt encourages her to step outside her *comfort zone* and accept a new career position. However, Dorothy is *content* and *complacent* with her current position, and living with her aunt and uncle. Though the outward appearance of a Phlegmatic is generally described as calm, cool, and collected, I chose Dorothy, as the Phlegmatic out of the four characters, so that I may address the areas of growth for this particular personality temperament. As she travels her journey of *the yellow brick road* and interacts with her friends she begins to display some of her strengths of a peaceful, patient, pleasant, friendly person and discovers her true need was a development and belief in self.

Some Related Characteristics between the Phlegmatic & Dorothy:
Supportive, helpful, content, and observant. Fearful, uninvolved, hesitant, timid, and doubtful.

Some Phlegmatic Weaknesses
 ~ Lack of Decisiveness
 ~ Hidden Will of Iron
 ~ Lack Enthusiasm, Energy & Motivation

Some Phlegmatic Strengths
 ~ Steady (free from change)
 ~ Calm, Cool, Collected
 ~ Pleasing Personality

Could you be a Dorothy or encountered her on your *yellow brick road*?

The Scarecrow (Sanguine Personality Characteristics)

The Scarecrow believes he needs a brain. Early on her journey, Dorothy is introduced to a *vibrant, talented personality* and performer with *creative fashion*, when she stumbles upon the Scarecrow in an abandoned field. Some oversized crows have reversed the Scarecrow's perspective of his purpose. Instead of the Scarecrow scaring crows, he becomes a victim of negative speaking degrading animals, who have convinced him he doesn't have a brain, and that he is only good for being their own personal entertainment. In spite of this ironic and disappointing situation, the Scarecrow remains extremely *optimistic* and *hopeful*, daily asking and *expecting* to be let down from "*this here pole*".

When Dorothy arrives on the scene - the day he knew would come - Scarecrow's face lights up as she scares off the crows and helps the him down from the pole. Falling flat on his face, he is *quickly discouraged, but just as quickly encouraged* by a few words from Dorothy. The Scarecrow shares he doesn't have a brain. However, Dorothy encourages (*Give support, confidence, or hope to someone*) and welcomes him to journey with her. Barely able to walk, Scarecrow *excitedly* helps Dorothy find the start of their *yellow brick road* journey to discover and obtain their hearts' desires as they '*Eased on Down the Road*', laughing.

Some Related Characteristics between the Sanguine & Scarecrow:
Optimistic, believes the best of people and circumstances, gullible. Unique attire, energized & enthusiastic, inspires others to participate, and experimental. Naive & gullible.

Some Sanguine Weaknesses
  ~ Forgets Obligations & Disorganized
  ~ Exaggerates & Excessive Talking
  ~ Naive & Gullible

Some Sanguine Strengths
  ~ Creative & Energetic
  ~ Fun-Loving & Appealing Personality
  ~ Outgoing & Optimistic

Could you be a Scarecrow or encountered him on your *yellow brick road*?

The Tin Man (Melancholy Personality Characteristics)

The Tin Man believes he needs a heart. As Dorothy and the Scarecrow skip and sing down *the yellow brick road*, they encounter a muzzled voice yearning for help. To their surprise, they find a tin man *frozen in position* on his back. After lubricating the *poor soul* with oil, they have compassion for him as he *sadly* expresses that he has no heart.

Dorothy and the Scarecrow listen, without interruption and with sincere understanding, as the Tin Man *depressingly* tells his story of how he was "abandoned" in the amusement park when it closed years prior. He further explains in *detail*, that though he had made *plans* for his future, he attracted "wrong" women with his *good looks* and *razor sharp wit* and was *crushed* in his prime when his fourth wife "failed him".

Regrettably, but heartfelt, he sings:

"What would I do if I could feel? And to know once again, that what I feel is real. What would I do if I could reach inside of me and know what it feels to say, I like what I see."

After experiencing, Tin Man's *self-deprecating* comments, "I'm a miserable hunk of junk", and soothing and lubricating him because he rusted himself with his *tears*, Dorothy and Scarecrow connected and convinced him there is hope as they welcomed him to journey with them down *the yellow brick road*.

Some Associated Characteristics between the Melancholy & Tin Man: Planner, intelligent, good looking appearance. Depressed, critical, feelings of abandonment, self-deprecating.

Some Melancholy Weaknesses
~ Easily Disappointed & Depressed
~ Excessive Preparation & Details
~ Remembers Negatives

Some Melancholy Strengths
~ Analytical, Cautious & Rational
~ High Standards & Ideals
~ Organize & Set Long Term Goals

Could you be the Tin Man or encountered him on your *yellow brick road*?

The Lion (Choleric Personality Characteristics)

The Lion believes he needs courage. Uplifted and excited, the three friends 'E*ased on Down' the yellow brick road* until they suddenly stopped to examine a lion statue that appeared to have eyes that were watching them. And thus, their encounter with the Lion; the mean ole lion, he declares as he breaks out the statue and *charges* them with his song of *power*, *intimidation*, and *threatening* sounds. With his 'let me conquer it, before it conquers me' mentality, Lion parades around proclaiming, "*I'm the king and don't get in my way because I'm here to stay; don't make me frown when you come around, because I will knock you down; I'm ready to fight day or night. And if I happen to let you slide, you better go run and hide because I'm a mean ole lion.*"

However, they quickly learn he is extremely fearful of many things as he reveals his secret; he doesn't have any courage. Of course, they invite him on the journey more confident than ever that they will find what they all are searching for.

Some Associated Characteristics between the Choleric and Lion:
Rises to the occasion in spite of fear. Overpowering, threatens with anger, fear of not having control.

Some Choleric Weaknesses
~ Bossy & Demanding
~ Impatient & Short Tempered
~ Insensitive

Some Choleric Strengths
~ Takes Charge Instantly
~ Make Good Quick Decisions
~ Goal & Task Oriented

Could you be the Lion or encountered him on your *yellow brick road*?

The 4 Personalities

None of us are 100% of any one personality. That is why we are all so unique. Though we may have similarities, no one is the same; like no one else shares your fingerprints, though they may share your name. You are unique!

Rather than label yourself, or others, as completely Choleric, Melancholy, Sanguine, or Phlegmatic, seek to discover the intricate details that make you who you are, and others who they are. That discovery will reflect a mixture in variations of *the 4 personalities*. Try not to live in your box of a category, expand your horizons into underdeveloped areas of yourself.

The 4 Personalities 'Eased on Down' the yellow brick road, encouraging one another, learning and gleaning from one another, and growing in the process. There's a part on the journey where Dorothy is singing to Lion, but it is as if she is also singing to herself and the others join in embracing the message for themselves as well. I believe the people that we attract is ultimately part of the journey that reflects an aspect in us that needs developing whether the encounter is perceived to be a good or bad one. In some strange way our relationships are reflections of various aspects of ourselves; whether it is an encounter for a moment in time or one for life. As it was with Dorothy, ultimately as she encouraged her friends, she herself was being encouraged and developing her need to believe in self.

Though your personality temperament may not identify with the Dorothy's character, we are all like Dorothy on the *yellow brick road* of discovering self and developing belief that we are *intelligent, caring, courageous* creations able to step *out of our comfort zones* to accomplish that which is in our purpose to accomplish.

As we embrace self, accept others and glean from personalities different from our own, we develop into a well-rounded person and discover abilities within that we did not know existed. Dorothy needed to believe, Scarecrow needed a brain, Tin Man needed a heart, Lion needed courage, and I needed to see; me. Like Dorothy and her friends, I discovered my potential was put inside of me by God from the beginning. And my encounter with others has developed my potential.

If you didn't realize it before, but always wondered why some people were so different from you, I hope this *Spittle* has helped you see you've been surrounded by *the 4 personalities*. I realized, "I was blind, but now I see".

Spittle #2

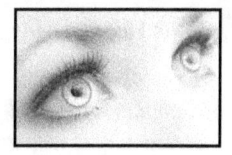

I WAS BLIND, BUT NOW I SEE!

Like *The Wiz* characters, we all have a need. I believe one of the best gifts given to me is spiritual insight beyond the surface of what the natural eye can see. Most of us don't realize we need to see things through the lenses other than our own natural eye. The ability to see not only from your own view point, but through the lenses of others and God's, really empowers you to be effective for yourself and with others. Often times we think that people are operating from our same perspective; or if they are not, we think they should be, otherwise something must be wrong with them - or something must be wrong with me. But God has shown me that **MUD** *Works* - **M**y **U**nique **D**esign Works! If I work it! And that goes for all of us.

Understanding the personalities allowed me to separate my feelings from a situation or encounter with another, and observe *the personalities*, including my own, interacting with each other. A personality is responding and reacting to what your personality is reflecting based on the characteristics of that personality.

For example, a Choleric respects facts & results, a Melancholy respects details & order, a Phlegmatic respects peace & quiet, a Sanguine respects joy & excitement. Therefore, you can position yourself accordingly to connect to the respective personalities so that you can obtain a desired result. Understanding me and what I am exemplifying, helped me to understand the responses I was getting from each of the personalities. When I did not like the response, I was able to reposition myself based on realizing what I was exemplifying and recognizing which personality I was encountering. Being able to see; see me, see others, see how people see me, and see how God sees me has been empowering.

Let's explore the story of the man born blind, and anointed by Jesus' mud spittle. His story parallels six steps from blindness to sight.

Jesus Heals a Man Born Blind

As he passed by, he saw a man blind from birth. And his disciples asked him, "Rabbi, who sinned, this man or his parents, that he was born blind?" Jesus answered, "It was not that this man sinned, or his parents, but that the works of God might be displayed in him. We must work the works of him who sent me while it is day; night is coming, when no one can work. As long as I am in the world, I am the light of the world." Having said these things, he spat on the ground and made mud with the saliva (spittle). Then he anointed the man's eyes with the mud and said to him, "Go, wash in the pool of Siloam" (which means Sent). So he went and washed and came back seeing.

The neighbors and those who had seen him before as a beggar were saying, "Is this not the man who used to sit and beg?" Some said, "It is he." Others said, "No, but he is like him." He kept saying, "I am the man." So they said to him, "Then how were your eyes opened?" He answered, "The man called Jesus made mud and anointed my eyes and said to me, 'Go to Siloam and wash.' So I went and washed and received my sight."

They brought to the Pharisees the man who had formerly been blind. Now it was a Sabbath day when Jesus made the mud and opened his eyes. So the Pharisees again asked him how he had received his sight. And he said to them, "He put mud on my eyes, and I washed, and I see." Some of the Pharisees said, "This man is not from God, for he does not keep the Sabbath." But others said, "How can a man who is a sinner do such signs?" And there was a division among them. So they said again to the blind man, "What do you say about him, since he has opened your eyes?" He said, "He is a prophet."...

So for the second time they called the man who had been blind and said to him, "Give glory to God. We know that this man is a sinner." He answered, "Whether he is a sinner I do not know. One thing I do know, that though I was blind, now I see." They said to him, "What did he do to you? How did he open your eyes?" He answered them, "I have told you already, and you would not listen. Why do you want to hear it again? Do you also want to become his disciples?" And they reviled him, saying, "You are his disciple, but we are disciples of Moses. We know that God has spoken to Moses, but as for this man, we do not know where he comes from." The man answered, "Why, this is an amazing thing! You do not know where he comes from, and yet he opened my eyes. We know that God does not listen to sinners, but if anyone is a worshiper of God and does his will, God listens to him. Never since the world began has it been heard that anyone opened the eyes of a man born blind. If this man were not from God, he could do nothing." They answered him, "You were born in utter sin, and would you teach us?" And they cast him out. (John 9:1-17, 24-34, ESV)

SIX STEPS FROM BLINDNESS TO SIGHT

1. Anointed with Mud Made from Spittle - *Knowledge & understanding of the personalities.*

Become aware of the different personalities in order to expand your knowledge and vantage points by obtaining and studying information from literature that specializes in *the personalities.*

Wisdom is the principal thing; therefore get wisdom: and with all thy getting get understanding. Exalt her, and she shall promote thee: she shall bring thee to honour, when thou dost embrace her She shall give to thine head an ornament of grace: a crown of glory shall she deliver to thee. (Proverbs 4:7-9, KJV)

2. "Go Wash"; Went & Washed. - *Willing obedience to instruction; going into the unknown and being willing to yield and be cleansed.*

Notice the man did not question Jesus' method or ask him what he was doing. He willingly obeyed to follow the instructions that had been given. Often people want to claim that the books, the tools, the information, the workshop, the church, the education, etc. does not work. When the truth is, it's more likely that the person did not do the most important ingredient of the process. And that is, you must willingly obey, walk into the unknown, or yield yourself; the way you do it, think it, see it, and feel it. You must be willing to do some difficult things - things you have never done before in order to get desired results.

3. Reflection - *I See Me*

I have seen this scene played out many times in Biblical movies. And the first thing that always happens is the man washes the mud off of his eyes, opens his eyes, and sees his reflection in the water. For the very first time he can see himself!

You cannot see yourself until you are face to face with an object that has the ability to reflect such as a mirror, or a pool of water - *or time with God reflecting*. Once you see yourself, you are able to see how God created you, your attributes, your flaws, and the mud that needs to be washed away. Your reflection allows you the ability to determine the modifications and adjustments you need to make so that you can accentuate and enhance yourself, while working on weaker areas of yourself. Reflection, or being able to truly see yourself, causes you to walk in confidence. You look the same, but different.

SIX STEPS FROM BLINDNESS TO SIGHT

4. Walking with Sight - *Seeing Others*

Once you truly see and understand yourself, you begin to see and understand others. Often I say, **MUD** *Works* because I can see me, I can see you, and I can see the muddy mess in the situation. After you have been anointed with the mud (**m**y **u**nique **d**esign)/personality understanding, and you have seen yourself, you then see the world, like you have never seen before.

You are able to identify what is true vs. what someone has told you is true. Then you are no longer negatively affected by others. You begin to stand up to what is truth and challenge what is not. But get ready! People will dismiss, disown, and disconnect from you if they are not ready for truth. Because once you have seen the truth in you, accept how you are designed and how you feel, you reflect the truth. You become a walking mirror, causing others to look at themselves, and then criticize you when they don't like what they see. *And they reviled him, ..."You were born in utter sin, and would you teach us?" And they cast him out. (John 9:28, 34)*

5. Positioning Yourself - *Seeing How Others See You*

It's amazing that other personalities are really just responding to what they see you reflect. Once you see the real you, you walk and talk different, because you see different.

~

The neighbors and those who had seen him before as a beggar were saying, "Is this not the man who used to sit and beg?" Some said, "It is he." Others said, "No, but he is like him." He kept saying, "I am the man." (John 9:8-9)

You can clearly see if a person respects who you are, by observing their reaction when you stand for the truth and against what is not. They will try to manipulate you to thinking something is wrong with you vs. taking a true look at themselves. And then speak more words of untruth. The "seeing" man was simply answering the questions, asking questions, and making comments according to his personal experience which was the topic of discussion. But they could not handle the truth.

The "seeing" man was not going to be persuaded, controlled, or manipulated into participating in the Pharisees judgments and accusations of Jesus, because he had been anointed, willingly followed instructions, saw himself, saw others, and was able to position himself against that which was not true.

SIX STEPS FROM BLINDNESS TO SIGHT

6. God Loves You - *Seeing How God Sees You*

Jesus heard that they had cast him out, and having found him he said, "Do you believe in the Son of Man?" He answered, "And who is he, sir, that I may believe in him?" Jesus said to him, "You have seen him, and it is he who is speaking to you." He said, "Lord, I believe," and he worshiped him. (John 9:36-38)

God loves you; for when people put you out, He will take you in. Don't feel alienated when you are "cast out". Rather draw closer to God so that you may believe; believe in Him, believe in yourself, and believe in the possibilities that there is hope for others to see too. Accept and embrace your unique design, clean up the mud in your life, and be confident in who God has designed you to be. Tell yourself, "*M*y *U*nique *D*esign Works! If I work it!

Spittle #3

MUD *Works*:
*M*y *U*nique *D*esign *Works*! If I Work It!

Mud has healing attributes to cleanse skin pores. Since ancient times, mud has been used in the treatment of a wide range of diseases; however, a number of people still shudder at the thought of having themselves smeared with mud. While many animals are known to roll about in the mud to get rid of external parasitic infestations, very few humans are willing to experiment with the same. This is largely because mud is strongly associated with dirt and filth, worms and bugs. Studies have found that mud does have beneficial effects on the human body.[1]

Watered dirt, mud, is the agent in which seeds/life grows. Clay, also known as mud, can be used to mold into beautiful and functional art work like pottery. Sometimes our personalities are like mud. They have good qualities but can get messy and no one wants to touch us. But if you are willing to "Go Wash" and spend time reflecting on what you see in yourself, you can wash the mud mess away. **MUD**: *M*y *U*nique *D*esign in its proper place cleanses, brings forth life and growth, and can be molded into a beautiful, functional work of art. If you face the mud in you, it can help you reflect and realize, **MUD** *Works*: *M*y *U*nique *D*esign Works!

In this *Spittle*, you will be challenged to understand and sharpen your personality. Let's explore the definitions of each word of this exclamation:

My - Saying something belongs to you. Belonging to or associated with the speaker; or relating to me or myself especially as possessor. Ownership.[2]

Unique - Being the only one of its kind; unlike anything else.[3]

Design - To create, fashion, execute, or construct according to plan.[4]

Works - Activity involving mental or physical effort done in order to achieve a purpose or result.[5]

My

Become aware, and take ownership and responsibility of who you are; your strengths, weaknesses, and tendencies. Embrace who you really are. Don't make excuses with yourself. Some things about you are not effective, but can be refined. If you know yourself, you can take ownership and create healthy boundaries and decisions that are suitable for your unique design.

Sanguine (Scarecrow), take responsibility that you can be forgetful, naïve, and believe a lot of things, even things that are not true because you have the tendency to think the best of people. Understand that everybody is not your friend and does not have your best interest at heart. And if you don't take time to think and strategize, you can be taken over by the overgrown crows of life. You are worth more than the entertainment for every party or occasion, but you also have a creative mind of optimistic influence.

Sanguines, you need attention from all, physical affection, approval and acceptance. And the source of your depression is a life without fun, no hope for the future, or feeling unloved. You are energized by people; therefore you must use wisdom and discernment and not be blinded and lost in your desire for people. Be mindful to not rely or expect *every person* to be part of fulfilling this emotional need and get yourself into a "crow" type of situation.

Melancholy (Tin Man), own up to the fact that "laying there in one position, (thinking, and pondering, and wondering, and figuring, and calculating, and re-thinking, re-pondering, re-wondering, re-figuring, and re-calculating) can make you tired!" And it can leave you lonely. Realize you may be connecting dots that everyone else is not connecting. Living in the valley of unforgiveness, bitterness, and hurt, will keep you stuck in time crying and "rusting" yourself, while others have left the scene. It may not be that others have "abandoned" you, but you decided to not move on with them or from them. This could leave you in a place of turning off your emotions so you won't get hurt again, leaving you believing that you don't have a heart. Your true heart of sincerity is received when you seek to connect vs. correct.

Melancholies, you are drained by people, withdraw from people as a stress relief, and become depressed if life (and people, including self) are not perfect. However, changing your perspective to see every imperfect person, place or thing that you encounter is part of the process to *perfecting* you in Christ Jesus, may be beneficial to you.

My

Getting an understanding of self and taking ownership of your needs, desires, and feelings, actually fulfills your needs, desires and feelings. However, not acknowledging your tendencies and people's response to your personality causes your needs to be unfulfilled.

Choleric (Lion), take ownership that you may have a fear of not having control so this may cause you to not trust others nor trust God. In effort to "conquer it before it conquers you", you may tend to intimidate, with your control technique of anger, dismissing, overpowering, and quick moving and talking. You don't have to always be on top, be first, be the best, or the loudest to still be King of the Jungle. Have the courage and confidence to allow others to be on top, go first or to lead. It doesn't make you less of a King. Have the courage to allow God to lead you into the unknown. And trust it will work out just fine. A true King is a servant leader who influences by demonstrating vs. demanding.

Cholerics, you have a need for loyalty, appreciation for dedicated service, and credit for good works, in addition to your need for control. You thrive on being in charge, and leading others. Beware of your quick moving, impatience and tooting your own horn that can turn people off. The same people that would follow you because of your great leadership and decision making skills, will also exile you from your jungle because people do not want to be ***controlled***.

Phlegmatic (Dorothy), take responsibility and ownership that not discovering, accepting and dealing with your feelings, nor others', causes disconnect from self, others, and possibly God. Though you may be quite content in this state, realize strengths to extremes become weaknesses, and too much of anything is not good for you. Being content in everything at all times can breed complacency and stunt growth. And though you think "you are fine" on the outside you begin to look like a shriveled up prune as life passes you by from lack of self growth. If you are not growing physically, mentally, emotionally, and spiritually, you are dying.

Phlegmatics, you have a need for self respect and worth, peace and quiet, and a stress free life. Therefore, you have very little desire to be around people, though they love to be around you. You tend to tune life out because you don't like to confront issues or be pressured to produce. ***But for self worth and respect you need growth, and for growth you need people.***

Unique

You are one of a kind. There is none like you. Therefore, the world and people need you. You have a purpose. And if you won't be you, no one else can. This same thing applies to every person that God created and designed. Therefore, realize others don't think it, feel it, see it, smell it, taste it, or will do it just like you.

Sanguine (Scarecrow), you are unique because without any effort you can bring energy and excitement to the atmosphere and truly show the world the joy of the Lord is your strength with your loving kindness and optimistic personality. You see life through optimistic lenses.

The possibility that today might be the day that you get down from 'this here pole'. {Scarecrows perspective in *The Wiz*}

You are naturally:

* Creative & Energetic
* Fun-Loving & Appealing Personality
* Outgoing & Optimistic

Melancholy (Tin Man), you are unique because without any effort you can bring sincerity, sensitiveness and fairness to the atmosphere, considering all angles and reflecting how your creator does things in decency and in order.

"I am known for my good looks (appearance) and razor sharp wit."
{Tin Man shares to Dorothy and Scarecrow in *The Wiz*}

You are naturally:

* Analytical, Cautious & Rational
* Have High Standards & Ideals
* Organized & Set Long Term Goals

Unique

*Be aware there is another unique perspective other than yours.
Don't take individual's unique personality personal. Accept it!
If you think "they" are peculiar, most likely
"they" think you are peculiar too.
Embrace your uniqueness and accept other's uniqueness.*

Choleric (Lion), you are unique because without any effort you can bring quick decisions and a victorious mentality to the atmosphere showing others that, "greater is He that is in you than He that is in the world".

"Keep standing strong and tall. You're the bravest of them all!"
{Words from Dorothy to Lion in *The Wiz*}

You are naturally:

* Takes Charge Instantly
* Make Good Quick Decisions
* Goal & Task Oriented

Phlegmatic (Dorothy), you are unique because without any effort you bring a pleasing friendly personality to the atmosphere, that calms, relaxes and supports others. *A man that hath friends must shew himself friendly: and there is a friend that sticketh closer than a brother.* (Proverbs 18:24, KJV)

"Do you want to come with me to meet the Wiz? Maybe he can help you too." {Dorothy's to Scarecrow, Tin Man and Lion in *The Wiz*}

You are naturally:

* Observant
* Calm, Cool, Collected & Consistent
* Pleasing Personality

Design

Be creative and strategize with what you know about yourself and others so you can be effective in your encounters with others. Don't take other personality styles so personal. Stay consistent and focused on the desired result and design a plan with your personality that doesn't manipulate or control, but that encourages and influences.

Sanguine (Scarecrow), you could have used your charismatic, influential personality to negotiate with the crows; barter freedom for your entertainment gift vs. giving so freely of yourself. Be mindful that you like to be the center of attention and are always "the life of the party". That attribute could help you design a more effective strategy with your creative capabilities. Instead, you befriended crows and allowed yourself to become a victim of "stinkin-thinkin" instigated by their negative comments about you, and convinced yourself you didn't have a brain.

~

Melancholy (Tin Man), you could have left the amusement park like your wife and everyone else left vs. allowing the closing of the park to become such a tragedy in your own personal life. Life happens, and though it may have been a tragic day, your razor sharp wit has the ability to create a new plan for your future. Instead, you mourned so long; you rusted and froze yourself in one position - one moment in time - while others moved on and "abandoned you" - as you see it - causing your heart to grow cold to the point you believed you didn't have one.

Design

Process your personality design before you respond. If you understand how people see you, you won't be as offended by them. People are reacting to what they see you reflect. Consider how others are designed, and connect to their inner needs vs. judge them because your design is different. Adjusting your approach doesn't mean that you are wrong, but you will be more effective and influential with your personality design.

Choleric (Lion), you could have approached Dorothy and the others and engaged them with your persuasive character when they discovered you were in the statue, and offered a "journey of a life time" to the Wiz since you are adventurous, resourceful, and bold. Instead you chose to overpower them with acts of intimidation, causing you to display the vulnerability you were trying to convince yourself doesn't exist. Allowing yourself to let go and let God is also a form of strength and courage.

~

Phlegmatic (Dorothy), you could have used the quality of being a good listener and support person, to listen to your own feelings, desires, and thoughts vs. being fearful, indifferent, and reluctant about change. Not allowing yourself to feel and see who you are causes you to not see your worth and causes you to not believe in yourself.

Works

Discipline yourself to not allow your strengths to operate in extremes so they don't become weaknesses, hinder you or become a muddy mess. You can adapt yourself in any situation. Find what you can agree with or connect with in another personality so they can hear what it is you are trying to communicate.

Sanguine (Scarecrow), without discipline, your entertaining stories can turn into nerve racking talking.

Melancholy (Tin Man), without discipline, your plan for excellence can turn into unrealistic expectation of self, life, and others.

Choleric (Lion), without discipline, your quick decisiveness and instant take charge ability can turn into you making impulsive choices, deciding for everyone, controlling everything, and manipulating your own way.

Phlegmatic (Dorothy), without discipline, your low-key emotions and easygoing, adaptable, pleasant, cooperative mellow personality can turn into you hiding emotions, blocking out feelings, and letting others decide; which causes you to refuse to budge.

Some Key Points in Making Your Personality Work

Awareness
Acceptance
Strategize
Discipline

Process / Observe / Study
Position / Think / Plan
Pursue / Talk / Connect
Produce / Work / Results

Adapt & Overcome
Be Mindful of Your Own Filters
Ownership of Your Temperament's Tendencies
Don't Take it Personal
Find something you like about all the personalities

Tell yourself daily, **MUD** Works - **M**y **U**nique **D**esign Works!
If I Work It!

Spittle #4

TOIL YOUR SOIL

Created from the Dust of the Earth

So God created man in His own image, in the image of God He created him; male and female He created them. (Genesis 1:26, NIV)

God saw all that He had made and it was very good. And there was the evening, and there was the morning - the sixth day. (Genesis 1:31, NIV)

The Lord God formed (designed) man from the dust of the earth (ground) and breathed into his nostrils the breath of life, and the man became a living being. (Genesis 2:7, NIV)

For you created my inmost being; you knit me together in my mother's womb. I praise you because I am fearfully and wonderfully made; your works are wonderful, I know that full well. My frame was not hidden from you when I was made in the secret place, when I was woven together in the depths of the earth. Your eyes saw my unformed body; all the days ordained for me were written in your book before one of them came to be. (Psalm 139:13-16, NIV)

Jesus spat on the ground, made some mud with the spittle and anointed the blind man's eyes and told him to go wash. The man went and washed, and then he could see. (Reference John 9: 6-7)

Isn't it interesting that Jesus (God in the flesh) used the same material, the dirt of the earth, to heal blindness. He returned to that which He created man with to heal man. He went back to his roots. That's what **MUD** *Works* (understanding the personalities) can do for you. It broadens your perspective of self, others, and God, and you realize you were once blind, but now can see in a way you've never seen before. The knowledge of this information, gives you wisdom and an understanding of why you do what you do as you reflect on your journey of life.

The reflection takes you back to your roots, and answers many unanswered questions about yourself and how you relate to others. Once you get to the root of who you are, you can toil your soil!

Getting an "A" in the Personalities - Toil Your Soil

To toil your soil means to work your **MUD** so that it is cultivated to reproduce good fruit. The first tool in toiling your soil, or working on your personality, is to learn how to glean from the strengths of the other personality temperaments. One approach to gleaning from all the temperaments strengths is what I call, getting an "A" in *the personalities*. *(To me, these following words that begin with the letter "A" have personality, so I associated them with the 4 personalities.)*

1. Get an "A" like the Melancholy (AWARENESS)
The melancholy temperament tends to research, study, and think; and likes the idea of being informed. Educate yourself and make yourself **aware** by studying and researching about *the 4 personalities* - the strengths, weaknesses, and tendencies.
My people perish for lack of knowledge. (Hosea 4:6)

2. Get an "A" like the Phlegmatic (ACCEPT)
The Phlegmatic personality tends to have attributes that accepts circumstances just as they are. **Accept** your unique design and don't deny it. **Accept** the unique design of others and don't reject or condemn it because it is not like yours. This is an internal process that you must push to make happen.

3. Get an "A" like the Sanguine (APPRECIATE)
The Sanguine personality tends to be optimistic about people and life, thus finding it easy to **appreciate** life and encourage people. Find something that you can agree with in each of *the 4 personalities*. Even if you find a small thing you can agree with, it will help you find aspects you can **appreciate** about them. When you are able to **appreciate**, you are able to make a connection, and it opens others up to hear your heart.

4. Get an "A" like the Choleric (ADJUST / ADAPT)
The Choleric personality tends to "adapt and overcome". After the internal processing has been done, the external work can begin. The Choleric personality likes to accomplish and achieve, therefore this step involves two A's. **Adjust** your *perspective* and *expectation* of the person you encounter after you have become aware, accepted, and found something to appreciate. And, **adapt** your communication style or approach for that personality.

Communication - Toil Your Soil

Connect vs. Correct

Often we seek to correct vs. connect when our personality is offended by another personality. However, if we stop, think and act, we can position ourselves effectively to reach a win/win situation. You won't be able to connect until you get an "A" in *the personalities*. If you react to your immediate feelings about the encounter, it may be a situation you will continue to revisit with that person. If all you want to do is get the person "told", that is all you will ever get. But if you want to make an influential impact, you first have to *toil your soil* before you can be infectious enough to influence someone else to change or grow. You have the right and the power to control your environment and how you are treated. But don't ever mistake this for the right to control people with correction. People will soon realize control when they see it, and will come from up under it. If you connect with people, they ultimately will listen and hear what you have to say.

> If they are a **Melancholy**, slowly give clear, precise details.
> If you are a **Melancholy**, give praise before criticism.
>
> If they are a **Phlegmatic**, show them respect, and encourage them that their opinion is important without interrupting them.
> If you are a **Phlegmatic**, practice speaking louder and sooner.
>
> If they are a **Sanguine**, smile and joy up the communication with colorful details, animated jesters, and sound effects if possible.
> If you are a **Sanguine**, allow others to speak and don't interrupt when another is talking.
>
> If they are a **Choleric**, give the results or bottom line first, and then go back and give direct, short details once asked.
> If you are a **Choleric**, request vs. demand, add "please & thank you", and actively listen without interrupting or completing sentences.

If this seems difficult, remember when you are weak, He is strong. You can do all things through Christ who strengthens you. *For I can do everything through Christ, who gives me strength.* (Philippians 4:13, NLT)

MUD *Works!* If you work it! And your seed will flourish into a tree or plant that others can pick from or cut from, and reproduce positive interactions with others.

Get to the Root of Who You Are - Toil Your Soil

Session 1 - My Unique Design
How are you designed? What is your function, your system? How do you process? How do you operate? The following are some questions & information to consider when you toil your soil.

1. The Personalities: Which personality/character do you most identify with? Are you more like a:

   a. Social Butterfly (Extroverted)
   b. Intentional Ant (Reflective)
   c. Barking Dog (Outspoken)
   d. Lackadaisical Turtle (Introverted)

   a. Sanguine: The Talker
   b. Melancholy: The Thinker
   c. Choleric: The Doer
   d. Phlegmatic: The Observer

2. Emotional Needs: What are your emotional needs & desires?

Which do you desire the most?
   a. to have fun
   b. to have perfection
   c. to have control
   d. to have peace

Do your emotional needs include?
   a. attention, affection, approval, and acceptance
   b. sensitivity, support, space, and silence
   c. loyalty, control, appreciation and credit
   d. worth, respect, no stress, and peace

3. Motivation: What motivates and excites you?

Do you often play, work, think, or observe first?

Do you like to do things the fun way, the easy way, the instructed way, or your own way?

Do you control the situation by charm, anger, procrastination, or moodiness?

Get to the Root of Who You Are - Toil Your Soil

Session 1 - My Unique Design *cont.*

4. Mixture: If you find that you do not possess all the attributes of the personality temperament you most identify with, that is because we each have our own mixture. Don't put yourself in a box. We are a mixture of all *the personalities* and should strive to be more like Jesus; who reflected all of *the personalities* in their strengths and none of the weaknesses. Aim to walk and live in your strengths and not your weakness.

5. Masking: Sometimes we consciously and sub-consciously mask our true selves as a coping mechanism to that which is uncomfortable to us. While this may work to help you through a tough time, ultimately a repeated action becomes like second nature and if you are not careful you will hide and lose yourself. You may get away from the unique design you were intended to be. This is why it is important to reflect on who you are and embrace the truth about yourself even if you don't like what you see. You may see a few mud spots. Willingly go wash. It is so much easier to walk around when you can see. But if you have blinded yourself for so long from yourself, you will be aimlessly existing and never completely walking out your power, purpose, passion or potential. For some of us, we have been blinded since birth and for others, we have been become blinded along the way. A mask not only keeps you hiding from others, but it keeps you hiding from self. And the truth shall set you free.

6. Nature & Nurture: We were all born with our own unique design, and our own unique experiences have affected and influenced our personalities. It is important to get to the core of who you are so you can determine where you are on the map and where you want to be. Whatever your journey has been, it is part of the process of you unfolding. And when you are ready, you can have your *anointed with a mud spittle experience* so you can see yourself in your reflections. You can see what is you, what is others, and what is just a mud mess that has been splashed on you during your journey. But when you wash, and continue to wash, what you are in your raw state can be refined. You will learn to love yourself and love others as God loves. Your *Nature* is what you were born with. Your *Nurture* is what has been given to you along the way to enhance you. You can choose, with every situation, if you will allow it to be an opportunity to enhance you like mud cleanses and grows, or if you will allow the mud to dirty you up.

Get to the Root of Who You Are - Toil Your Soil

Session 2 - Works
What is your contribution or your purpose in life and how do you plan to accomplish it? The following is a check list when you toil your soil.

1. Create a Personality Plan by practicing various responsible responses.

2. Build your self-esteem and confidence level by getting an "A" in *the personalities*: **A**wareness of yourself; **A**ccept yourself; **A**ppreciate yourself; **A**djust your perspective and expectation of yourself and **A**dapt and overcome your challenges.

3. Accentuate strengths and minimizes weaknesses.
Live in your strengths vs. living in your weakness.

4. Adjust your communication style for each personality: do you need to be direct, quiet, detailed, funny

5. Notice the Clues - but ask questions to get the true personality.
`Sanguines have attention grabbing voice *(Smiley Face)*
`Cholerics have a stern walk and direct tone *(Stern Face)*
`Phlegmatics are in a relaxed mode of operation *(Relaxed Face)*
`Melancholies are deep in thought or processing mode *(Serious Face)*

6. See how you and others fit in the puzzle? Every personality is needed.

The Melancholy thinks before doing, but sometimes thinks too long. The Choleric acts first and thinks second, but may have to redo. The Phlegmatic observes before responding, but if observes too long, opinions may not be considered. The Sanguine brings excitement to the room, but if too much fun, purpose won't be fulfilled. So all *the personalities* have a place in the puzzle and is needed for complete effectiveness. Phlegmatic, observe the situation, Melancholy make the plan, Choleric carry it out, Sanguine, encourage the love and joy. Glean from each:

My = Phlegmatic *(be hopeful)*
Unique = Sanguine *(be creative)*
Design = Melancholy *(be strategic)*
Works = Choleric *(be productive)*

Believe this... **MUD** *Works*! If I work it!

Spittle #5

YARD CRASHERS

There is a reality show my husband and I watch on the HGTV network called *Yard Crashers*. There's a team of landscapers that would walk up to people while in a home improvement store, solicit their trust and ask if they could come to their home to do a yard makeover. It was funny to watch some people dodge the head-hunter, while others found them quite humorous and believed it was a joke. Once the Yard Crasher Crew (YCC) located their person, they would consider all the elements of the person/family's needs, desires, and preferences and create a unique design with their dirt. Some of those yards were nothing but dirt without any life in them at all. The points I gathered from this show were:

1. The YCC sought after their prospects, and the people never saw the blessing coming. Similar to the blind man, Jesus anointed the man with mud made from spittle not because the man sought after Him, but because He reached out to the man. God reaches out to us through people, be He is often rejected.

2. The first thing the person had to do is "let go" and trust the experts to give their yard(dirt) a makeover from all the wear and tear it had been through, or allow them to create a new design from a yard of dirt. We must let go and let God (the expert) give our dirt (mud) a makeover, as He takes us back to our original design.

3. The YCC adjusted perspectives and expanded horizons. They unexpectedly took people off their original agenda. We must allow God to take us off our agenda so He can adjust our perspective and expand our horizons.

4. The YCC spent time helping the people see exactly the yard they needed to meet their needs, desires, and preferences. We must stop and make ourselves available for God to show us what is inside of us so He can guide our yard to be designed in a way that satisfies our needs and desires that He created us with.

5. Some yards were full of dirt with no life at all. You may need to have a Yard Crashers Experience (an experience with God, the expert) if your yard (personality) is only a yard of dirt (mud).

6. Some people avoided the crew. We must not be like those people who dodged the YCC. For we will miss out on a brand new yard that meets every need, free of charge by the expert designer - Jesus.

Seeing Life from the Other Side of the Fence

Yard Personification
For fun, let's describe *the 4 personalities* using yards as a analogy.

1. Sanguine Yard. A yard full of colorful flowers and fun activities like pools, swings, grills, table & chair lawn sets, and entertainment items - representational of Sanguines because they like to have fun.

2. Choleric Yard. A nicely manicured yard with a lawnmower, shed, and other yard tools like shovels, rakes, etc. - representational of Cholerics because they like to work.

3. Melancholy Yard. A yard with nice, neat, sectioned rows of fruits and vegetables - representational of Meloncholies because they like nature, organization, and details.

4. Phlegmatic Yard. A yard with a shaded lawn chair without much of anything else in the yard - representational of Phlegmatics, because they like to keep cool, relax, and are content with being by themselves.

The Choleric Yard looks at the:
Sanguine Yard and says, "Too cluttered."
Melancholy Yard and says, "Too much planning."
Phlegmatic Yard and says, "Too lazy."

The Sanguine looks at the:
Melancholy Yard and laughs, "Too serious."
Phlegmatic Yard and laughs, "Too lonely."
Choleric Yard and laughs, "Too much work."

The Melancholy Yard looks at the:
Phlegmatic Yard and thinks, "No purpose."
Choleric Yard and thinks, "No life."
Sanguine Yard and thinks, "No silence."

The Phlegmatic Yard looks at the:
Choleric Yard and looks away.
Sanguine Yard and looks away.
Melancholy Yard and lays back in the lawn chair.

Imagine how differently you might see, if you came out from your yard, and looked at your yard from the other side of the fence.

Spittle #6

LOVE

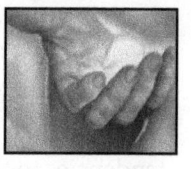

In the story of **The Wiz**, first referenced at the beginning of this journey, the main character Dorothy sang a song as she reflected of her journey of *the yellow brick road*. She reflected of the different world, and the different people, and the friends that she encountered along the way. And in some strange way, while she was an encouragement to them, they in return were a reflection of different aspects herself. Their experience together allowed her to grow and develop, and obtain her specific need on her journey, to believe in herself.

The part that speaks volumes to my soul is her communication with God:

*"Suddenly my world's gone and changed its face, but I still know where I'm going. I have had my mind spun around in space, and yet I've watched it growing. Oh. If you're listening God, please don't make it hard to know we should believe the things that we see. Tell us should we run away, should we try and stay. Or would it be better just to let things be? Living here in this brand new world might be a fantasy, **but it's taught me to love**. So it's real, real, to me. And, I know that we must look inside our hearts to find a world full of love like yours, like mine, like home."*

Like Dorothy, looking inside, seeing and understanding me gave me a greater appreciation of myself and the desire to see, understand and give people the same kind of grace and mercy that God gives to me daily. We see our relationships through our own lenses. As I have discovered, friends and family see the relationship through their own lenses, also. The perspectives are usually different. So, there are elements of the relationship that may be real and others that are simply a matter of perspective. But as Dorothy said, rather it's real or not, it has taught her to love. And that is my story; I choose to embrace the journey, my encounters, and my relationships and appreciate the growth and development that each has taught me. In essence, it has taught me to love; love myself and love others.

God is love. And He first loved me. [Ref. 1 John 4] *There is no greater love than this, than a man who would lay down his life for a friend.* (John 15:13, AMP)

I like to look at laying down my life as yielding my personality tendencies to the circumstance or person at hand in a way that causes me to walk in love and truth and brings positive results. Jesus reflected all the personalities in their strengths, and He was what He needed to be when He needed to be it. We have learned in ***Spittle 4*** that we were made in God's image. Therefore, we too can be what we need to be, when we need to be it. Like Dorothy did.

When Dorothy and her friends came to the end of the *yellow brick road* and arrived at the Emerald City to meet the Wiz, through intimidation, the Wiz demanded that only Dorothy come up to see him. However, Dorothy, laying down her life (personality tendency), was not going to leave her friends behind; for they too had traveled a journey to fulfill their needs. I also see this as wisdom, and not letting go the growth and development (her friends) that she obtained on her journey. But she kept pushing forward towards the goal!

In order to receive their requests, Dorothy was instructed to kill Evilene by the "fake" Wiz - who believed she would kill Dorothy first. Though afraid, Dorothy decided to face her fears, and her friends decided to stick by her side and adapt and overcome their fears too. Scarecrow, Tin Man, and Lion all represented some part of Dorothy and her overall disbelief in herself. But as she traveled the journey, and encountered friends to love, she developed in the process to overcome her fear. For they all started their journey with some type of fear, as we all do, but that spirit is not from God. *For God has not given us the spirit of fear; but of power, and of love, and of a sound mind.* (2 Timothy 1:7 AKJ)

TEAM = Together Everyone Achieves More
No Fear - Dorothy. *Power* - Lion. *Love* - Tin Man. *Sound Mind* - Scarecrow

---

Together they took off to take over the enemy, and feared no evil. *Behold, I give unto you power to tread on serpents and scorpions, and over all the power of the enemy: and nothing shall by any means hurt you.* (Luke 10:17, AMJ)

Yes, though I walk through the valley of the shadow of death, I will fear no evil: for you are with me; your rod and your staff they comfort me. (Psalm 23:4, AKJV)

There is no fear in love; but perfect love casts out fear: because fear has torment. He that fears is not made perfect in love. (1 John 4:18 AKJ)

Through love, Dorothy and her friends were able to cast out fear and confront evil. The evil one will always try to steer you away from your journey and your purpose. Knowing that **MUD** *Works* gives you the strength to keep pressing toward the goal that the Lord has for you. They discovered the Wiz was a fake, but the journey of the *yellow brick road* did bring them to a place of discovering self. Dorothy encouraged her three friends, "*Believe in yourself right from the start. You have brains, you have a heart. You have courage to last your whole life through. If you believe in yourself as I believe in you.*"

Dorothy was wise to free her friends with the truth of what was inside of them all along. Dorothy was led to realize the same was true for her with this statement, "*Home (her desire) is a place we all must find. Not just a place where we eat and sleep. Home is, knowing your mind, knowing your heart, knowing your courage. If we know ourselves, we are always home, anywhere.*"

Dorothy had the power to go "home" all along by clicking (tapping) her heels three times; symbolic of she had everything she needed, as it is with us. [Tap into the three manifestations of God: Trust the Father, accept Jesus the Son as Lord and Savior, and allow the Holy Spirit to lead you and guide you in all truth]. "*You will know the truth and the truth will make you free.*" (John 8:32, NLV)

Though she had the power the entire time, the *yellow brick road* journey allowed her time to process and to discover this truth. We usually want to get to the end result with our personalities, our relationships, and our encounters; but we miss the process. The process of growth and development the *yellow brick road* offers; an encounter with *the 4 personalities.*

Sometimes we think we are doing good, operating in our gifts, and helping people in the name of love. But I believe an important part of love is found in Ephesians 5:21, *yielding one to another*. [To hold yourself back and allow another the right away for the betterment of the situation; for example preventing a personality crash.] Love is seeing the heart of the person and desiring to connect with them vs. correct them; it's believing in them. That kind of love changes lives. Dorothy connected and saw in her friends what they didn't see in themselves.

1 Corinthians 13 gives the template to **Love** no matter which personality temperament is dominant in you.

> Though I (Sanguine) speak with tongues of men and of angels, and have not **Love**, I become as a sounding brass or a tinkling cymbal. And though I (Choleric) have the gift of prophecy, & understand mysteries & knowledge, and though I (Phlegmatic) have all faith, so that I could remove mountains, and have not **Love**, I am nothing. And though I (Melancholy) bestow all my goods to feed the poor, and though I give my body to be burned, and have not **Love**, it profits me nothing.
>
> **Love** is patient and kind, encouraging and not jealous, unpretentious and not boastful, humble and not arrogant, respectful and not rude, selfless and not selfish, forgiving and not provoking, thinks good and not evil; does not rejoice in iniquity, but rejoices in the truth;
>
> **Love** always protects like a Choleric, **Love** always trusts like a Sanguine, **Love** always is hopeful like a Phlegmatic, **Love** always perseveres like a Melancholy. **Love** never fails!

Our journey is not just made up of our friends and family, but also of encounters with those that appear like our enemies for various reasons. As I mentioned, looking inside, seeing and understanding me gave me a greater appreciation of myself, and allowed me the desire to see and understand and give others the same kind of grace and mercy that God gives to me daily; even if it appears that they are against me. *But I say unto you, Love your enemies, bless them that curse you, do good to them that hate you, and pray for them which despitefully use you, and persecute you...* (Matthew 5:44, KJV)

God/Jesus represents *the 4 personalities* in their strengths and none of their weaknesses. **Love** causes you to dig deeper into **your** dirt, even spit on it and make mud; smear it on your eyes, wash your eyes so you can see yourself clearly, see others the way God sees them, see how others see you, see how God sees you, and then position your personality in a way that is influential and causes you to walk with the confidence that **MUD** *Works*!

I hope these *Spittles* - little eye openers - have given you new perspective and a new way of seeing. So toil your soil and let God crash your yard while you are on your *yellow brick road* journey, because He **loves** you and others too. **MUD** *Works*! If you work it!

Commitment

Make a commitment today to dig deep into your soil, and discover the intricate details of your personality. Wash away the mud that you may find. Then, walk in the true love of your personality. Write down the mud you need to wash away so that you can say, "**MUD** *Works* - **M**y **U**nique **D**esign *Works*! If I Work It!"

Notes

Introduction

1. "Reflection." Wikipedia.com 2013.
http://en.wikipedia.org/wiki/Reflection_(physics)
(Accessed April 29, 2013)

Spittle 1

1. "Brick." Wikipedia.com 2013. http://en.wikipedia.org/wiki/Brick
(Accessed April 30, 2013)

2. "Yellow." Wikipedia.com 2013. http://crystal-cure.com/yellow.html
(Accessed April 30, 2013)

Spittle 3

1. Team Healthizen (2010, September 1) "Healthy properties of mud." Healthizen.
Retrieved from http://www.healthizen.com/blog/index.php/general/healing-properties-mud/

2. "My." Wikipedia.com 2013. https://www.google.com/search?q=my
(Accessed April 30, 2013)

3. "Unique." Wikipedia.com 2013 http://www.thefreedictionary.com/unique
(Accessed April 30, 2013)

4. "Design." Wikipedia.com 2013. http://en.wikipedia.org/wiki/Design
(Accessed April 30, 2013)

5. "Works." Wikipedia.com 2013. https://www.google.com/search?q=works
(Accessed April 30, 2013)

About the Author

Natalie Shanel Watts

Natalie, in her educational pursuits has obtained a Bachelors of Arts in Art & Design with a minor in Communication, Certified as a C.L.A.S.S. Communicator (Christian Leaders, Authors, & Speakers Seminars) and a Personality Trainer through CLASSeminars, Inc., which has trained over 30,000 men and women; and to her credit is a recipient of an Honorary Doctorate in Christian Education.

After her 7 year career in the Forms Design industry, she founded Younique Design, Inc., specializing in custom designs with a purpose. She also has a strong desire to help people understand their purpose and uniqueness; therefore, expanded her business and started **MUD** *Works* - *M*y *U*nique *D*esign Works!, which provides workshop services to help people become effective in any relationship by understanding themselves and others. In addition to **MUD** *Works*, Natalie has also authored a children's book, *The Creative Crayon Color Party*, that can be used to encourage children's uniqueness, and co-authored with her husband, *11:11 What Time Is It?*, a book for married and engaged couples on understanding the power, purpose, passion, and potential in the marital union.

Natalie and her husband, Robert, are from the Chicagoland area, and are proud parents of a beautiful daughter. They serve as Elders and Marriage Ministry Leaders at Family Christian Center, where senior pastors are Dr. Steve and Melodye Munsey. As founders of One Flesh Ministries, Inc., a ministry focused on building strong marriages and families, they host classes and gatherings, which incorporate *The 4 Personality Styles*.

Visit **www.youniquedesign.biz/menu** for more information on custom invitations & programs, children's books & workshops, couple's books & classes, and **MUD** *Works* workshops.

WORKSHOPS

MUD *Works* for your church. In the church environment there are often many ministries and groups of people organizing different functions or activities. Learning *the 4 personalities* can help you approach people in a way that motivates and not discourages them. Church is a place where people most want to feel safe and loved by all, and there is a great expectation to meet emotional needs. Understanding how others are designed, will help you in demonstrating love in a unique way to each individual, and build teams of unity and fruitfulness.

MUD definitely works! A couple of years ago, Natalie taught a series to some key leaders on my team which yielded tremendous results. We were able to identify and accept one another for who they were while realizing that it was ok for them to process and think differently. **MUD** *Works also allowed us the opportunity to understand the different personalities within our team and learn how to problem solve and work more cohesively as a group!*

Winter Dojcinovski
Artistic Director, Family Christian Center

PERSONALITY PARTIES

MUD *Works* for a fun time learning the 4 basic personality styles. This two-hour introduction to personality styles is offered to those who want to expose their circle of family, friends, and foes to personalities in a fun-filled, lighthearted environment. Usually, personification is used to describe the 4 personality styles. Personality Parties are designed to be fun, but educational, and give people an awareness of themselves and others too. The purpose of these parties is also to encourage people to be able to laugh a little more about our differences vs. judging, condemning, and correcting our differences.

Book a Private **MUD** *Works* workshop or party at your place, or to get on our e-mail list: **contact@mudworks.biz**

PERSONAL CONSULTATIONS

MUD *Works* for your personal one-on-one training. These consultations can help with individual relationships by answering specific questions about your personality as well as others around you. This private time helps you to apply the principles of the personality understanding to your individual life. It is more beneficial for the Personal Training to follow a **MUD** *Works* Workshop, however it is not required. The first session must be a minimum of two hours. Every other session, set by appointment, will be charged in half-hour and hour increments.

Phone consultations are also available for your convenience. You may make appointments on an as need basis. Personal Training is highly recommended and services people the best.

If personality consultations were a drug......I'd have to say that I'm addicted. Natalie is so passionate about personalities and I found myself tugging at the information out of my own frustrations in some of my personal relationships. I absolutely LOVE the one on one consultations and they have helped me resolve some issues and help me know how to deal with and relate to people according to their unique personality style......which I am discovering is more effective!

I see myself being a life-long **MUD** *Works customer!*

Tamike Hurley

MUD *Works* also for schools, businesses, park districts, seminars and more. **Visit www.mudworks.biz** for more information.

For Your Information

For more information on the study of *the 4 Personalities*, the following are recommended books:

Wired That Way by Marita Littauer
Your Spiritual Personality by Marita Littauer
Personality Plus by Florence Littauer
How to Get Along with Difficult People by Florence Littauer
Communication Plus by Marita & Florence Littauer

Below are other books published by **Younique Design, Inc.** that encourage you to embrace your uniqueness, accept differences, and discover your purpose.

The Creative Crayon Color Party
by Natalie Shanel Watts

11:11 What Time Is It?
{It's time to recognize the Power, Purpose, Passion, & Potential in your union?}
by Robert & Natalie Watts

Children's Book & CD

Couple's Book

PERSONAL CONSULTATIONS

MUD *Works* for your personal one-on-one training. These consultations can help with individual relationships by answering specific questions about your personality as well as others around you. This private time helps you to apply the principles of the personality understanding to your individual life. It is more beneficial for the Personal Training to follow a **MUD** *Works* Workshop, however it is not required. The first session must be a minimum of two hours. Every other session, set by appointment, will be charged in half-hour and hour increments.

Phone consultations are also available for your convenience. You may make appointments on an as need basis. Personal Training is highly recommended and services people the best.

If personality consultations were a drug......I'd have to say that I'm addicted. Natalie is so passionate about personalities and I found myself tugging at the information out of my own frustrations in some of my personal relationships. I absolutely LOVE the one on one consultations and they have helped me resolve some issues and help me know how to deal with and relate to people according to their unique personality style......which I am discovering is more effective!

I see myself being a life-long **MUD** *Works customer!*

Tamike Hurley

MUD *Works* also for schools, businesses, park districts, seminars and more. **Visit www.mudworks.biz** for more information.

For Your Information

For more information on the study of *the 4 Personalities*, the following are recommended books:

Wired That Way by Marita Littauer
Your Spiritual Personality by Marita Littauer
Personality Plus by Florence Littauer
How to Get Along with Difficult People by Florence Littauer
Communication Plus by Marita & Florence Littauer

Below are other books published by **Younique Design, Inc.** that encourage you to embrace your uniqueness, accept differences, and discover your purpose.

The Creative Crayon Color Party
by Natalie Shanel Watts

11:11 What Time Is It?
{It's time to recognize the *Power, Purpose, Passion, & Potential* in your union?}
by Robert & Natalie Watts

Children's Book & CD

Couple's Book

www.ingramcontent.com/pod-product-compliance
Lightning Source LLC
Chambersburg PA
CBHW061300040426
42444CB00010B/2442